Naked Reflections:
Insights from a Wise Soul

Charles D. Patton

Cover Photo: By Book Design Company

DEDICATIONS

Thanks to all my family and friends for
Constant Support, to "authoreva" at fiverr.com for her editing
services and positive feedback, to Dr. Geoff K. Patton
for final edits, and to my wife, Estella, for final word check.

Table of Contents

Peace

Why Is Peace Important?

Because no one should impose their beliefs on others,
no matter how strongly they believe others are misguided.

Because no one wakes up wanting to be hurt or killed,
and no one should wake up wanting to do that to others.

Because war never produces happiness for anyone,
in the end, no matter the outcome, no one wins.

Because NOTHING, I mean NOTHING, is worth dying for,
unless protecting yourself and others from bodily harm

Because ideology is infeasible beyond a single individual,
meaning, no two people will EVER agree on EVERYTHING

Because compromise is the best solution for disagreements,
any time more than one person is involved.

Because it all starts with one person thinking that their
ideas are better than those of another, but they never are.

It all ends either with Understanding or Suffering and Death.
Abandon power, ye mongers, and leave us all live in peace.

Our World is a Mess

Condors soar at the edge of natures' existence
while kitties chatter at caged canaries.

Great mammals beach from submarine sonar
while Japanese call whale murder food research.

Exhausts block sunrays; that melt the ice, warm the earth
while ultraviolet beams cause skin cancer.

Children can't play in their yards for fear of molesters
while the Internet foists our worst on curious Muslims.

We consume food in excess and support many addictions
while we tolerate greed from both legal and illegal drugs.

Nuclear Neanderthals negotiate to join the Big Boys Club
while being a "Beast" is a compliment to some but not most
Arabs.

Movies inject the worst ideas in youthful minds
while the extreme religious ban books and take over School
Boards.

Does anyone still care about mankind, truth,
freedom, peace and the health of our world?

Charles Patton

Children Could Save the World

If only the savage beasts of the world
could have a three-year-old child to love,
to watch, to teach and help grow.
How could a true father kill others
and look his child in the eyes?

Charles Patton

Peace Will Forever Elude Us

Humans can't stand much boredom,
they abhor emotional vacuum.
They crave mental stimulation.

Depending on their situation,
they will drift in different ways,
Creating emotional activity.

A President might start a war,
because he feels a need to create
a way to prove a political point.

A child may throw a tantrum
to create excitement and attention,
just for being ignored.

Humans loathe simple peace and quiet.
Except a rare few like the Dali Lama
and those who survived the horrors of war.

Gratitude and Love

Stardust

In my eyes and in my heart,
love lays down a coating
of magical dust,
capturing the fingerprints
of our passing time
and waiting to be cleaned off one day
far in the future.

My Guardian Angel

I rejected religion in college, once I learned better.
However, there, I also met my Guardian Angel.
If that sounds contradictory,
Let me assure you it is.

Religion calls on people to accept tenets on faith.
College teaches you to accept only the facts.
Catholicism believes in Guardian Angels…
nothing could be farther from facts.

But, in my case, without faith, I have one.
Now, some people might say that my angel
is a mortal woman, and others my wife.

But I would argue she certainly is angelic,
and has watched over me like the best Archangel.
Truly, I would be dead if it wasn't for her.

From keeping me out of war to
helping me to kick the deadly habits
of nicotine tars and alcohol.

But more than that, she has literally
saved my life, and made for me a life
I would never have had, and that's a fact.

Charles Patton

Love of My Life

My wonderful wife taught me to read.
Well, actually, the nuns taught me how.

My wife taught me the love of it,
She taught me to want to read.

Charles Patton

Home, 1974

A tender wife,
our lovable dog,
not a bit of strife.

A weird fish,
the warm TV,
a broken dish.

Open year 'round,
squirrels in the yard,
vegetables in the ground.

Warm in the winter,
a place to hide,
care for a splinter.

Comfort and ease,
cozy and safe,
to sleep, walk or tease.

Charles Patton

March 21, 1964

The ultimate in love
is to have one woman
and she only you.

March 21, 2014

The penultimate in love
is to stay with that same woman
and she with you.

March 21, 2024

Beyond the best in love
Is to still have each other
After 60 years

Charles Patton

How Do I?

How do I tell you that I still
love you after so many years?
How do I tell you, when I've already
told you in so many ways?

After so many years, of laughter and tears,
how do I convey how I truly feel?
Even though I've said it
every day, in every way, since our first day.

Charles Patton

How Long Ago Was Paris?

Love of art mingles with our love for each other,
      as we strolled the city.
Some of the greatest delights of our lives,
      spending time together,
as we've done for so many years since.

"Til death do us part" has real meaning,
      to us an unbreakable promise.
An easy commitment when we find something nice
      that we both love to do.
Our love for art continues strong as we go along.

Our love grows every year like a tall redwood tree,
      never bending, ever strong,
steadily evolving and spreading its canopy as it matures,
      with seemingly endless life.
As majestic as the finest art we love so much.

Nature

Charles Patton

Bothersome Questions

Red-crested woodpecker,
        brightest color in the aviary rainbow,
alights on the ground, strange for an aerial
        jack hammerer.
Unusual visitor to such terrestrial solidness,
        this redheader.
Perhaps he's picking up work dropped from above.
Clumsy?

Queen Ann's Lace, a beautiful weed.
If you look closely, you'll see, in the very middle,
a single tiny dark purple floret.
Why is that there? Whose idea was that?

I have killed plants by overwatering them,
yet, other plants live and thrive in water.
Bacteria live their lives in hot steam undersea,
and we boil medical instruments to sterilize them?

Charles Patton

On the Edge of the Pond

On the edge of the pond, the great blue heron
stalks the unseen. The S-curve of his neck is still,
narrow and smooth, as a gently bent branch.
Then, suddenly, he explodes in a lunge.

In his beak, my wife's favorite large bullfrog
wriggles his last and in a flash, a lump appears,
inside that smooth tubular passage,
and ever so slowly, lunch is served.

Charles Patton

The Last Quiet Place on Earth
(An Ode to Peace and Quiet)

I grew up deep in the city
among sounds of trucks and sirens,
amidst my neighbors' wailing babes,
and TV commercial slogans.

No quiet could I find between
the clacking of the subway and
the whine of gears and children,
steady torment by urban sounds.

Mechanical sounds of the city
pierced every wall surrounding me,
entered every corner, my ears…
I found no urban quiet.

I ran, first chance, to the country,
only to find gurgling brooks,
and chirping cicadas,
interrupted by the bull frog's "glump."

Car tires scratching on gravel roads,
planes droning in the distant sky,
farm machinery turning up the dust.

The absence of noisy quarrels,
with the very nature of humans,
with our breaths, sniffles, and gurgling guts.

Far remoteness didn't help,
a deep cavern in the Wyoming Rockies,
delivered droplet drips and shuffling shoes.

At the top of Kilimanjaro, not there,
glaciers cracking, stones falling, panting,
and thunder in the distance.

A mountain monastery where I prayed
for contemplation in solitude,
a choir practiced behind some unseen door.

No matter how remote I went,
the core elements conspired:
wind, water, fire, and earth.

Add to them, animals and insects,
unharmonious choir that they are,
and quiet is chased away.

Add technology and mankind's
modern conveniences to the mix,
and noise pollution is defined.

A couple of near-misses,
music and meditation
come as close as can be.

When music plays and
blocks out all other sounds,
leaving one pleasant one behind.

Meditation comes closest
for the few who can manage
to calm the noises in their mind.

Seeking the acoustic vacuum
seems a possibly impossible quest
and a lonely one at that.

Peace is not quiet and
quiet is not peace.
Quiet will come when we die.

Hopefully, we find peace before
and learn to live with the best of
our favorite neighborly noises.

White Vision

Gazing out my frosty window,
I see a sight of snowy white,
perched three quarters of the way
up a majestic tulip tree.

From my cozy room,
I look out upon woods now
becoming stark as winter drifts in
upon my surrounding world.

I can see black trunks crowned
with misty gray twigs,
reaching like tiny cracks
into the dark and cloudy sky.

Standing wide amidst
an interwoven field of evergreens,
so tall and thin,
this brave tulip tree.

With its leaves hanging on,
gradually turning a reddish brown,
but still holding on tight
to the place of their birth,

Like we who hang on
to this precious earth,
as we wrinkle and fade
with hope for at least another day.

And sitting on the front line
of this leafy brigade of brave,
yet battle-losing, leaves rests
an unlikely white visitor.

How exciting it would be,
if it were a wispy ghost, but that's
too unusual for this pastoral place.
Vision of a grand white wonder.

Well, not totally white, but nearly so.
A saw-whet owl, a rare Virginia sight
only three ounces with a big attitude.
A beauty to perfect this winter scene.

Seagulls

Nuisance or necessity.
So many varieties,
colors of white, grey,
white with black heads and more.

The garbagemen of the sea,
and garbagewomen of the sea.
Cleaning the gutters where
the tides meet the sand.

They float, they fly,
They walk, a little wobbly.
They stand on posts wherever they are,
and will steal your bait when they can.

And when you are not looking,
they may leave their mark on your hat.

Charles Patton

Nature's Clean-up Role

Rain scrubs the earth clean,
washing our debris to the sea,
Wind blows our fumes around
and ruins our lungs.

Trees are losing their fight
to clean up our mess,
while forest fires confound
the air that we breathe

Our water's no safer
from the misdeeds of man
with our discarded trash
and effluent streams.

Nature can only do
so much to clean-up
And when we exceed her limits
What next will we do?

For drinking and breathing,
keys to us staying alive,
what will remain,
unless we refrain?

Charles Patton

Eraser

The ocean's the world's greatest eraser,
erasing our beaches, twice every day.
Millions of footprints gone with no trace,
along with sand castles big and small.

Sometimes at sea, the ocean arises
to erase an entire ship with its crew.
At times, it has done its job so well
that no sign remains for others to find.

When the ocean fully awakens,
it has been known to erase
an entire city without any grace,
removed for good from the earth's surface.

And if the ocean felt especially mean,
it could erase an entire country,
gone for good without any warning,
with no remorse and no recollection.

Charles Patton

On the Beach

I will sit on the beach
and let the tide come to me.
I will wield the power that
gravity gives us all, see?

The tide here comes twice a day.
It has no choice, option or say,
but I know within it lurks
the power to sweep me away.

Sitting on the beach, I see
a small skiff motoring by
with two unknowing riders,
silhouettes against the sky.

I hear the soulful sputter
of its single old putt-putter,
pushing them toward home and life,
unless it fades and dies.

Miami Marriott

I see before me,
next to the pool, just before night,
a tree of yellow flowers,
absent any leaves, they'll come later.

Monochromatic fireworks,
a wondrous sight, I sit and watch,
to imprint on my mind
its glorious aerial image.

Charles Patton

I See God

I see God in the heart of every flower
and in a child's smiling face.
I see God in frightful atomic power
and in every mother's grace.

I see God in my wife's eternal love
and in Arlington cemetery.
I see God in every sparrow and dove
and in marvelous new machinery.

I see God in creative imagination
and in mountains, low or high.
I see God in magnificent musicians
and in any piece of pie.

I see God in those who dignify the old
and, in warm and cheerful hugs.
I see God in crystals, trees, and mold
and in the smallest yucky bugs.

I see God in a baby's eyes ablaze
and in a furry cat's soft paw.
I see God in storms that last for days
and in a baby tiger's claw.

I see God everywhere
and you're blessed if you do too.

Gems

If you walk toward the setting sun
on Chesapeake Bay beach, along the water's edge.
And, if you're a lucky one, you might just find
a small treasure; an amber-colored stone.

Your stone will be polished dull but clear,
enough to allow light to glisten through,
tumbled in the washing machine of waves and sand.
It may not be perfect; it may not be round.

But it will be pretty, this stone you found,
and it will be free, and it will bring good luck,
and it will be yours to keep for all your time—
unless you give it to someone you love.

Charles Patton

How Lucky Am I?

To have heard the waves roll down the beach
in perfect rhythm with the sea.

Like hearing the beat of my heart
or the wings of a honey bee.

To have watched them rise then curl and
crash in perfect symmetry.

Like seeing the Blue Angels fly
or geese cruising in their formal vee.

To have heard nature's symphony
of sounds in perfect harmony,

Like a great orchestra playing
their best piece in the ideal key.

To have tasted the briny air
in perfect accord with my favorite tree.

Like enjoying a part of life,
most people never get to see.

Charles Patton

Slow Walkin' Dog

Who can describe,
a young dog gone old

That once jumped, ran,
swam, fetched and rolled.

Who can describe
this graying muzzle

That now goes slow
yet tries to hustle.

The bark's still there,
ears and nose aware.

But eyes mistake,
and limbs don't bound.

Dog doesn't sense
how those seeing care,

Slow walkin' dog's
still walking around.

Social Commentary

Charles Patton

The Bounty

I am awed every time I enter a grocery store,
Or, God forbid, a Sam's Club,
at the vast wonderland of material goods,
all within reach of most Americans
who have no clue how lucky they are.

The plenty, the cornucopia, the variety,
food fresh, frozen or canned.
10 kinds of Preparation H – who knew?
Enough calories to feed an Army for months.

Can we not share some of this
                with the rest of the world?
Why do we deserve so much,
                while others get so little?
One "storeful" per month from each state
would feed a million or more, I'd bet.
And, we wouldn't even miss it.

The Kindness

Poor lonely college kid
working, studying, not very well,
eating lunch in the same café every day.
Kind old navy vet behind the counter
serves him the same every noon:
pork sandwich and a shake
and only charges $ .57,
while others pay $2.57. Why?
Because he was kind.

Some people have empathy,
others feel nothing for others.
Does one learn to care
or is one born sensitive?
I think you learn as a child.
I think you learn from your mother.
I think you learn when you suffer.
I think you learn by feeling what others feel.
With feeling, you can become kind.

Charles Patton

Putin

Putin is evil,
a killer in power.
Orders men killed,
keeps his hands clean.

He invades countries
that don't want him near.
He supports dictatorships,
to justify his own.

An egomaniac maniac,
the ultimate psychopath
with no redeeming value,
no good for our world.

I hope Hell is real.

Philosophy

Charles Patton

The Fuzzy Edge

I want to live on the fuzzy edge,
where there is no black or white.
I want to live on the fringes,
where rules are mine to write.
I want to live on the edge of time,
where sanity meets insanity, winking.
I want to live on an untouched planet,
where nearby stars taunt me, blinking.

I want to live in the crazy zone,
where art runs naked and wild.
I want to live outside my fenced in mind,
where nothing is known, and anything is possible.
I want to live beyond my means,
where my desires outrun their fulfillment.
I want to live within my means,
where living to excess can be found for free.

I want to live at the children's playground,
where silly ideas abound.
I want to live among unexpected thoughts
where no idea can be anticipated.
I want to live as a three-year-old,
where truths are known, and inhibitions are not.
I want to live outside the norm,
where animals talk and children play.

I want to live where no one lives,
where new thoughts take me to new places.
I want to live without responsibility,
where such freedom truly sets me free.
I want to live where everything is fresh and new,
where my needs are simple and yet still few.
I want to live where no one is notable,
where everyone is better than everyone else.

I want to live among the fearful,
where running for my life inspires.
I want to live among the fearless,
where nothing stands in my way.
I want to rise above all else,
where the view exceeds my horizon.
I want to rise above my destiny,
where my footprints will be remembered.

The Core of Our Existence

Birth, Family, and Death are
the straight and narrow of our lives.
These three legs of our stool define
our beginning, middle, and end.

We arrive, we relate, we care, and we leave.
So simple, yet maximally complex.
The center line of intermittent conflict,
and the source of our worst pains.

Family is nuclear and vertical and
biological and adoptive – It makes
no difference how a batch of us
come together into a connected whole.

All that matters in this world
is how we are born, treat others, and die.
Not "how" as in the means,
but as the root of our character.

We can only hope to be well-born,
and well-bred as we awake.
But we have power while we live,
over how we live and even how we die.

And though the odds favor that
we won't choose when we die.
We may get the choice of how we handle death.
Will a life of grace teach us to die with dignity?

When I die, please tell my family
that if I did not die with dignity,
it was my wish to have done so…
Is there even a drop of dignity in that?

Why Are We Here?

All my life I wondered why we exist.
Early on, I felt it was about feeding desires,
Then, I thought it was about raising a family.
But, in the end, I discovered the truth of the matter.

We are placed on earth for one reason
and only one reason, one that is easily forgotten,
to do the only meaningful thing humans can do,
which is to **relieve the suffering of others.**

This usually doesn't mean giving away money.
It means being there when needed,
                              being that ultimate friend,
and relieving their pain and helping them grow and
filling the holes in their hearts when they're sad.

It means feeling their feelings and
                              reading their thoughts,
knowing their challenges and
                              helping them find their way.
Rarely, it might mean saving their life
                              or preventing their harm.
Often it is simply listening and holding their hand.

Mankind's highest purpose is to relieve others'
                              suffering.
Our duty is to help the next person in need
                              that we encounter.
If each person does their duty,
                  Mankind's purpose is fulfilled.
Leaders, strive toward this goal, and
                  the world will be at peace.

Man Doesn't Last

When Adam first became aware,
what he must have seen
and what that growing brain
must have learned and realized.
Did any of his thoughts survive?

No Man lasts very long.
Maybe a few of his thoughts,
if he puts them down, remain.
And too few of those
Are worthy for decades.

Who Am I?

How can I be truly philosophic
when I've scarcely suffered at all?
I never walked the fiery coals
of burning love rejected.

I've never lived under the despot's foot,
and had my rights deprived,
I never felt the sting of causing the big loss,
and ending up in second and total unknown.

I've never been the starving artist,
or the Parisian bohemian gone wild.
I've never lived among the poor,
or suffered violent storms at sea.

So what rights can I claim to have,
to share my point of view,
on important matters that affect our lives,
when others have lived much more?

Charles Patton

An Idea

I am an idea, whose time has come
I fight to emerge from my cocoon.
When I do, despite my beauty
I am judged by the non-creators.

Some will try to collect me,
claim me as their own.
Some won't see my true soul.
A few may see my worth.

Visionaries may augment me,
while most will tear me down.
If I'm truly worthwhile,
I will grow legs and fly.

Much too often,
even when worthwhile,
I am criticized to death or
ignored 'til I fade away.

Haiku

American Haiku

Old black and white cat,
hearing outside bird twitters,
hums primitive sounds.

      Crows cackle and caw,
      stark against newly lain snow,
      in no rush for spring.

            Ripples from my stone,
            sea waves to infinity.
            Silent greeting sent.

Plump red strawberries,
tart flavors waiting to burst.
My open mouth waters.

      Grey-faced Labrador.
      Old man walks barely ahead.
      Both dream of their youth.

            Wild wind blowing south.
            Mallards fighting to fly north.
            A close contest won.

Boys skateboard down curbs.
An old woman disapproves.
Frowns have no effect.

Star shoots in an arc.
Where's it from, where does it go?
Wishes go with it.

Man dresses for sleep.
Old dog puts herself to bed.
Love lurks between them.

Pipe, slippers, family dog,
Favorite nostalgias grow old.
Spring blossoms anew.

Air pours from the sea,
so pure, so clean, taste free.
Feels fine deep inside.

Jungle canopy,
hiding unknown bugs, chirping,
waiting to be found.

Crystal blue water.
Balmy breeze cooling hot skin.
Whole body soothed.

Iridescent green,
levitating hummingbird,
hypnotizes me.

New technology,
so many useless features.
baffles even me.

Gentlewoman's hand,
massages my aching feet.
What could be nicer?

Alto, contralto,
tenor, soprano, and bass
lift me to heaven.

Yo Yo Ma's so good.
Music that makes me happy.
Cello is my soul.

A feast for my eyes,
beautiful woman dancing,
and she is with me.

Pretty little stones.
Into my pocket they go,
beauty fades at home.

Sounds of birds abound,
twitters, tweets, whistles, and chirps.
No word names them right.

Green and slimy pond.
Frogs sing and frolic unseen.
Music to my ears.

My tension rising
from awaiting my dear bride.
When will she arrive?

Snake's tail disappears
inside a small hollow log.
Don't think I'll follow.

Chatter in my head,
distracts me all day and night.
Wish I could shut up.

My house is my home,
by my wife's design and touch.
I wouldn't be elsewhere.

Feelings are fragile,
many easily broken.
Be more sensitive

Cypress tree so tall,
standing with knees in water.
You must like it so.

Little yellow bird,
free and wild canary.
Wind in your feathers.

Cat nears lying dog.
Big black dog growls.
Cat kisses dog.

Breeze sways the prairie grass,
in waves of grain, tawny and tan.
Dry grainy aroma.

Mushroom Haiku

Mushrooms erupting,
so many colors and shapes.
Dangerous mysteries.

Red-tinged mushroom,
size and shape of a small plate. Certain deathly
taste.

Fungus on dead wood,
white on top, grey underneath.
Crescent-shaped canvas.

Filament fingers
standing shoulder to shoulder.
Like leery lemurs.

Mysterious force,
pushing up the summer ground.
Launching fertile spores.

So many colors,
yellow, red, brown, white, and grey.
Nature's pure palette.

Charles Patton

Messages

Charles Patton

Modern Poetry

I distain cutesy poetry
that spreads words across the page
in odd and distracting ways

Creeping configurations
with vague thoughts
unconnected from one to the next

Disconnected from any
matters that matter, leaving me
with only one feeling, antipathy

Immigrants

Polish cab driver, American immigrant,
how quickly you adjust.
Been here fifteen years but tethered still to home.
Been back 12 times since.

Hardworking, real estate entrepreneur,
focused, unmarried, supporting his parents.
How his life will continue to change as
hard work makes the difference.

Talented tailor and smooth salesman
talked me into better style than I imagined.
First person I ever heard to say,
"In America, it is so easy to make money,
but it is so hard to hold onto."

Big Change Comes Hard

Official misconduct roils my gut.
So many people have no clue.
Worse, those who have a clue, don't care.
Some care but fail to act from comfort or fear,
reluctant or unwilling to step forward.

A few step forward meekly,
to be shouted down or ignored.
Rarely a person clarifies truth so perfectly,
so clearly that others wake up, follow their lead,
and join together to effect change.

Assassination so often follows.

Charles Patton

Fact or Fiction

Who can tell what's true or not?
A fact today can evaporate tomorrow;
A tale of yesterday can become fact today.

Travelling to the moon was once a tale.
Ulcers are caused by stress was once a fact.
Every day science fiction becomes real.

If truth can't be told with certainty,
and if fiction can become reality,
then why care which is which?

Charles Patton

Live a Safe Life

Place yourself nowhere near volatile gas.
Boilers can explode with no warning.
and propane can burn your house to the ground.

Bring nothing into your home
that might spew carbon monoxide,
an insidious and silent killer.

Don't overload circuits, or
use a metal knife to clear a toaster, or
mix water and electrical appliances.

Don't climb ladders higher than
you could survive from a fall.
And don't touch power lines with metal ones.

Don't cut wood on a table saw
wider than its length,
Better, get one with auto-stop.

And always keep a hand
On the handrail, it's there for a reason,
Watch where you step, inside and out.

If you are right-handed and cutting,
watch your left hand, as that's always
the one cut when you slip.

Never cut toward you
And never leave pot handles
sticking out where you walk.

Never assume a baby can't move,
because when you do, they will.

Charles Patton

Our Time

How we value the time God gave us
amazes and confuses me.
Some of us dull our senses with
booze or drugs to bypass time,
others zone out on books or TV.

A few spend a lot of time
at live amusements, like sports,
and some spend time with their kids.

A few of us spend time trying to create,
and even fewer of us succeed.
Which way of spending time is best?

How you spend the time you're given,
is a decision you can't take back.
In an instant each second is gone.

Some don't think about time at all,
pushing such thoughts beyond their mind
with any numbing alternative.

Some depend on minds of others.
A few explore what's in their own,
and a few mine revelations.

But, in the end, your time is short,
solely under your own control.
Live to have no regrets at all.
So when you shuffle on, you will
have left not one second wasted.

Inspiration

You know when you get it,
you know from where you got it,
But "from where you got it,"
rarely knows you got it where you did.

If you got it from someone special
and you let that person know,
you will amaze and please
and complete a fine circle.

Charles Patton

Poems

Poems come from the mind of one
to affect the minds of many.

The best leave indelible marks
on the behavior of mankind.

The worst leave no shadow and
flee the dawn before the sun rises.

Some break the trains of our thoughts,
others obscure lines, stir feelings.

A few play tricks and make us laugh,
the worst make us sad, like their authors.

Words are often chosen more
for their obfuscation than clarity.

Modern ones use contrivances and
aim to be stranger than ever.

When they get strange enough to please us,
how many will we then remember?

The Game

If you are one of those few who still smoke,
if you buy into the glamour of drinking wine,
if you revel in your morning cup of Starbucks,
you have bought into the Game.

Addiction is the cash cow,
                            the source of most wealth.
While not the cruelest form of slavery,
                                that's what it is.
They have you by your vices,
                            and you can't escape.
You have no idea how good you would feel
                                if only freed.

But, probably never will before you turn to dust.

Charles Patton

Everyone Needs to Feel Valued

What would happen if no one wants
the best you have to offer?
Will you starve? Will you die?
What if you have no options? None at all?

Will you, out of desperation, commit crimes?
or strike out on a new path or homelessness?
What if you are too old, is your future hopeless?
Is it true, old dogs can't learn new tricks?

Can you, will you ask for help?
Will anyone help? What if you have no one to ask?
And, if someone tries to help, will it really help?
We all need to feel valued.

Can you find someone you can help?

Me

Choosing Me

"Spectate" or participate,
Recurring choice throughout my life,
To sit and watch or get out and play,
Be passive or aggressive.

Observe or checkmate,
Recurring choice between peace or strife,
To stand by or join the fray,
Be inactive or reactive.

Deadweight or teammate,
Recurring choice of spoon or knife,
To safely cheer or risk the throws,
Be the captive or the native.

Dictate or narrate,
Recurring choice of bear or bare,
To sit with friends or fight with foes,
Be in the crowd or on the team.

Placate or heavyweight,
Recurring choice of here or there,
To get soft and sad or hard and glad,
Be someone else or just be me.

Charles Patton

Farm Talk

We talked about farms today.

Farm work is the most satisfying.
At the end of day, every day,
you can stand back and see all
that you did for your day's pay.

Farms, for all their charms,
have their own unique aromas,
that follow you home to
remind you of manure and hay.

And, farms have their own terms.
We argued round and round 'bout
Shucking or shelling
and 'tween 'shalks or stalks.

I will always talk about farms.

Charles Patton

My Life

I have lived tough
and I have lived easy.
Whether poor or rich,
ignorant or wise,
I have lived well,
and enjoyed my life.

Dark Shadows

Dark shadows creeping across my lawn,
as clouds moved past the bright moon,
out of sight above the house.

My mind raced around what I have done
and the forces coming, leaving me with
the simple choice of death or defiance.

To die by my own hand, or face grinding,
degrading, even abject, ridicule
for the rest of my life.

To die at the top, leaving unanswered questions,
or be thrown down from the pinnacle,
is not a sane choice.

But, when I consider how
my long-gone mother would feel,
to have her life's reputation dashed

And be abandoned by her dearest friends.
And, to mark my children forever,
leaves me with only one choice. Bye.

Charles Patton

White Crow

My Indian name is White Crow--
White for good luck and
Crow for my intelligent craftiness.
I'm told I have Indian blood,
so I felt the need to name myself.

White upon the black, still earth,
cawing for its protection,
making it safe from waves
of row houses sweeping
across the land.

Perpetual Motion of the Mind

A stream running too fast to see one's reflection,
out of control, out of its mind,
on its mad dash to the sea, no matter the obstacles.
Attempts to divert it are feeble, at best.

What marvelous outcomes could be had
if one could direct the power of that stream
to worthy and rewarding endeavors,
and leave behind thoughts of value?

Charles Patton

Alone

Have you ever been lonely…
really lonely?

A single dingy room
off a dark, grimy hallway,
shared bathroom
down the hall.

In a strange and dangerous big city…

No friends, no neighbors
that you'd want to know,
Landlady peaks from behind her door,
you'd better be alone.

And don't forget the weekly rent…

Window view of solid brick.
Waken every night when the bar below
breaks liquor bottles in the dumpster.
An old radio upstairs plays sad songs,

Hot plate but no TV,
your only company.

Charles Patton

Laughter

Everyone likes to laugh uncontrolled.
Some laugh at jokes when they're well told.
Some laugh at me when I trip and fall,
while crazy ones laugh at nothing at all.

Some laugh all the more as they grow old.
I want to laugh but not when I'm told,
Some laugh every day, at every chance,
I want to laugh but by happenstance.

Charles Patton

My Brain

Not that I really want to,
I live on the logical
left-hand side of my brain.
I fight to be on the right,
but it always fights me back.

I crave to be creative.
I long to be like Longfellow.
I resist what I do best.
What is easy simply bores me.
Why is that? Yes, why is that?

I'm most good at connections,
systems and numbers are me.
I seek the arts and beauty,
beyond my need for order.
Why do that? Yes, why do that?

Should I abandon my strengths
for what is likely a whim?
How can my talents align
with what I prefer the most?
Will I know? What I will be?

Life's a natural rhythm
as people speak their words.
We seem to speak in sevens.
Must be there are as many
gods above as in the heavens.

Charles Patton

My Building

My building is falling down around me.
Its roof, faded and grey, has some bare spots.
The siding has cracks, creaks, and wears thin.
Its useful life dwindling down to *has been*.

Inside it's almost as good as new,
just a bit tattered here and there,
but the exterior is past the point of renovation,
and there are no renovators to be found.

It's as if termites are drilling their holes,
gradually weakening its very structure,
or the sheer force of nature playing me
with its cruel game of extreme entropy.

Historic preservation is not an option,
no tax credits for this place, not a one.
Demolition and reconstruction is also no-go,
Resignation seems the best road to hoe.

When my building was young and newly built,
it was strong and beautiful and felt alive.
Now, it doesn't know how long it has been,
and no clue as to how bad it has become.

One day soon, he will come strolling along,
the demolisher, with his fork and tong.
It may happen in a sudden bang, but
there's no stopping ultimate consequences.

My Parents

Unlike some siblings, I don't blame my parents
for what I am or what I have become.
Sure, they taught me to argue too much, and
they passed to me their alcoholic genes.

But along the way, I've had many other
opportunities to take different paths,
to make my own decisions, good or bad.
So, the fault can't be mom's or dad's, just mine.

Parents hope their influence is for good,
setting what their kids will someday become,
but their influence can only reach so far.
Sometimes, kids turn out far better or worse.

Grandparents probably do more to form
the foundation of what kids will become,
Blending gentle persuasion with setting
examples of what is best behavior.

Unlike strict parents who feel great pressure
to control, limit, and apply their rules
and sometimes use more force than needed.
For all they try, they have little effect.

Reality is that playmates and peers,
with the playground bullying they applied,
did more to move me in important ways
than my parents did on their best of days.

Charles Patton

Logic Land

Logic Land is where I dwell,
'tis not the place I want to be.
It forms for me my private hell,
Trapping me from being free.

Specters swarm in Logic Land,
touching me with an ethereal hand,
haunting my haunts; trapping my soul,
demanding more order than I can stand.

As a resident of this Land, I live a narrow life,
striving constantly to prevent any strife,
while simultaneous, synchronous, omni-directional
time travel is what I need, with my wife.

While deep in my tortured mind,
                  I crave creative byways,
stretching in all directions at once like hay,
where music, art, and literature intersect
and philosophy is served in teacups along the way.

Yet here I sit enmeshed as I am
in analysis and emails. I want to scram,
while I wonder why I can't be free and
why every thought I have is a diagram.

If I Were Only

If I were to work harder, then I could be wealthy,
but most people who work hard never get rich.

If I were rich, then pretty women would surround me,
but none would love me as does my beautiful wife.

If I were a golfer, then I would meet important people,
but then I would spend less time with those I truly love.

If I were really smart, then I could be
                                    our country's president,
but then I would have no peace
                        of mind and constant worry.

If I would only exercise more and eat less,
                                then I would look good,
but I would be often sore and miss the joy of fine food.

If I would only practice, then I could be perfect,
but just to practice won't make me talented.

If I would just stay the way I am, then I should be happy,
but I never seem to be satisfied with my own status quo.

Poor Is Relative

Poorness is less rampant now than in eras past.
Being poor, centuries ago, exceeds our imagination.
History tells of the horrors of starvation and death.

Poor today, in America, compared to that,
is less onerous, but even our poorest are better
than many of the poor in India or Africa.

Yet, poor is never good for those affected,
not that being dirt Poor from the start
has anything good to say about it.

But, a poor person will feel worse
going from being well-off to losing it all.
The distance fallen amplifies feeling poor.

My poorness may not be as poor as most poor.
Going from having every comfort to wearing hand-me-
downs,
and having my self-confidence crushed by bullies.

Being poor affected me deeply.
but not as a result of being poor,
but by the reactions and actions of others.

Charles Patton

Am I a Coward?

More than once in my life,
My true character revealed itself.
Everyone wonders how they will react
when a calamity calls upon them.

They say heroes happen
when someone runs toward danger
rather than runs away, or
freezes weak-kneed.

I think anyone might be heroic,
in one case, but not in another.
Being heroic depends on
what someone stands to lose.

Would you risk a loved-one's life to save another's?
Being a hero is hard because it demands
quick decisions and instant risk-assessment,
which no one trains for, and most are poor at.

But being a coward is easier.
It requires inaction or avoidance.
Repercussions can be severe or
nothing at all if no one knows.

Was I a coward once when offered
by a farmer to watch him slaughter a steer,
or when I turned away when my father
dispatched a pig with a baseball bat?

Was I a coward again in Africa
when the guide told me that if I were to
step out of our open Land Rover,
the male lion 12 feet away would kill me?

Again, was I a coward when
I climbed to the top of Kilimanjaro
hiking to 19,500 feet with a guide,
rather than doing it alone?

Being a hero or a coward turns on judgment,
good commonsense on one knife edge,
and shame, embarrassment or death on the other,
Before you judge a coward, know them.

Awonder

I was born awonder,
agog and blank as slate.
Then I grew to question,
to learn and relate,
until I began to fade
and it became too late.
In the end, I lost my filters
and much I came to hate.
When I go, I'll lose my masks,
and take all the love with me.

Charles Patton

Fate

Big Fat Dog

Age sits on my chest like a big fat dog,
A Saint Bernard licking my face
with heavy breath, fogging my eyes.
Weight that slows me from my prior pace,
I await the day the big dog gets off
when I'll be moving with wings of lace.

When did you first appear?
You came out of a haze.
Now you get fatter every moment,
feeding off the treats of my waning days,
consuming my every breath, my very routine.
I have become your chaise.

Your mass grows with each opportunity
that comes, and I let pass by.
You feed yourself from my tray of time
with a sickly joy. You are not shy.
Get off me, fat dog. Let me live my life!
While you make me weak and make me cry.

The weight you add as I lose mine.
I rail against your heaviness.
I will enjoy what I have, while I still can,
as you suck life from me, no less.
And yet, you increasingly grow in bulk and burden,
leaving me more and more a mess.

I will ignore you, as much as I can, but
my strength fades as you gain, turning me to clay.
I know you will grow faster and faster.
Go away and come back another day,
but still, I push you back.
I will live while holding you at bay.

You disturb my consciousness more and more,
Becoming by the day increasingly brash
and scaring me witless as you do.
You hear no command and feel no lash.
There's no repulsing you, you dumb cur.
Go away and leave me alone before I crash!

If I ignore you, will you stay away
                                 a few more years?
I will keep fending you off 'til
                               my last drop of blood
and when I can no longer resist,
                               I know you'll creep up,
and on that fatal day, land on me with a thud.

Random Images

My road undulated ahead as far as I could see,
converging in the distant light
                          to a pinpoint of nothingness,
but where my tires touched the earth,
                               it rode like a waffle.

My destination, my fate,
my purpose aimed to live in the moment.
Miles of mammals, days of dreams.

Choirboys in red robes chant Gregorian sounds.
Incense smoke swirls and seeps directly
into primitive corners of my brain.

What am I experiencing?
Meditation, blind faith, divine bliss
                    or simple delusion…
I can't tell, but who really can?

Charles Patton

My Abyss

She's a gossamer veil,
rising out of the sea as
a wisp of white fog,
enveloping my soul

She's so fickle,
swimmin' laps around
the edges of my world,
as I know it.

She's moody,
running dark some days
and sparkling on others,
then the sun shines.

She runs deep and
can be shallow.
She ebbs and flows
with an irregular rhythm.

She gives birth and death
with equal measure, and
when she kills,
she lives on without remorse.

Full of beauty and
a master of disguise.
When she is high, she terrifies;
when calm, she soothes.

At home in the Hadal Zone,
she possesses evil whimsy.
No one knows
what Fate will do next.

Provoking

Charles Patton

Colt Terry
(A real person)

A first Green Beret
and smaller than most.
As brave as could be,
and not one to boast.

Grateful for being
so many times, spared.
Remembered so well
by those that he saved.

Reckless in deeds
but not without care.
Always a back-up plan,
he would prepare.

He loved so many,
in the manliest way.
Married five times, cared
for each wife, he'd say.

Fathered two children,
who knew naught of him.
Yet he risked his life
for us and them.

He lived as a soldier
each and every day.
He loved his non-coms,
led them in every way.

Charles Patton

He killed those men,
who would have killed him.
Hoping the memories
would eventually grow dim.

He trained and fought hard.
First to volunteer, never shy,
and from Agent Orange,
he eventually did die.

Given all we asked
of him to do,
he gave us his all.
Had we even a clue?

When he went to his Maker,
leaving us behind and free
to enjoy our lives and loves
to be what we can be.

He fought for us,
leaving many spared.
At least when he died,
those who came cared.

Fruits of my Thoughts

My thoughts bulge, ready to burst
like milkweed pods in the fall
to seed an unsuspecting world,
riding the air to who knows where.

Carried on a gentle stream,
seeking soil on which to land,
taking root where 'er they may, or
falling barren upon hard ground.

Those that take root then become
fresh sprouts bursting with new life
to repeat the cycle with more
new thoughts and compound creations.

On the Edge

Between water and air, and air and space,
and oil and water, and crystals and air,
and solid and liquid, and rock and gas.
There lie important mysteries
where atoms of different kinds
meet and choose to not join hands.

Greek and Latin

Cicero and Methuselah may be lost,
For now and forevermore.
Today's youths are being
taught more "practical" skills.

Big-thinking school administrators
concluded years ago, that teaching
"dead" languages was passé,
and instead, teach skills for dying trades.

Reading Plato and Aristotle is
no longer logical or de rigueur.
And reading in the original Greek,
as Jefferson did, forget that.

Upon what basis
will our future leaders
appreciate and defend
what our fathers founded?

Reviving "dead" languages,
would bring back to life
what our forefathers knew,
when forming our country.

How will our youth understand,
not just the past, but the
great ideas and grand visions
that formed our great country?

Who among our youths
will be the next great thinkers,
and what knowledge will they have
to formulate new ideas or protect the old?

Charles Patton

Wall Street Workers

Name for those who produce little
but endless computations, hedges,
deals, disclosures, and derivatives.

Farmers at the end of day
can stand back and see the
immediate results of their labor.

Bails and pails, meat and milk
roll off their assembly line
ultimately to feed the world.

But Wall Street workers,
what do they give the world
at the end of their shift?

Mostly nothing more
than money for them and their bosses
skimmed off the hard work of others.

Greed is an ugly life's goal,
but it seems to be innate
in too many self-centered Humans.

Obscurity and Obfuscation

Blisters on my aching limbs,
fallen weak to my side from
baloney and bullshit.

Crapola, monsignor,
the messages you hyped were
lies leaving jagged wounds.

Ring lifelong in the ears of
the used, abused and misguided,
among past trusting followers.

Putrid puke upon thou,
who ground the true faithful
beneath their lustful feet.

Where went the truths
once believed – a butterfly gone,
back to Caterpillar but squashed.

Charles Patton

Miscellany

Charles Patton

The Letter "P"

Pshaw and phooey,
puckish and peevish,
phenomenal peripatetic,
poverty struck,
so Pathetic.

Manufactured Mystique

Pool bars, raw bars,
couples & men,
imbibing, enjoying,
all cozy in their den.

Scooble Scarble
(new words for our vocabulary)

Pockers and plooks,
smakes and smoots,
coincidingly with chiprose.
Phine and propase,
ribbled and floutile,
floodle with vergre.
Whather rotisserated or smuffered,
replicatable or gelled,
I like all these expecially.

Russia

Seems everythin'
written 'bout Russia
is lengthy and wise.
Well, this isn't.

Sudoku

You just keep coming,
grabbing my attention,
imprisoning my mind,
consuming my time.

You entice me,
annoy me and,
too rarely satisfy me,
yet too often defeat me.

Macho Man

Never does a guy feel lonelier
or more like a real man,
than when his woman says she will stand
behind whatever decision he makes.

Charles Patton

When Is the End the End?

Now!

ABOUT THE AUTHOR

Charles Patton, MBA, RRP, is an award-winning Author and prolific Business Leader who spends his winters in Florida and his summers in Illinois. After his extensive travels, he stumbled upon numerous muses, from Mother Nature to diverse cultures and the people behind them. Ultimately, these adventures across the globe birthed his passion for poetry.

He is an accomplished writer of non-fiction, fiction, plays for film and radio, and newspaper columns. Texas A&M University Press published his first book, *Colt Terry, Green Beret*, in 2005. He also researched extreme leaders to produce his book on *Extreme Leadership*. Published by the American Institute of Management Science (AIMS) in 2013 for its course in Leadership, and republished in 2024 as *Extreme Leadership* is currently ranked 395th on Amazon among Management Science titles. He also published in 2017, under AIMS, the title, *Thinking*, a compendium on the subject of using your mind to better yourself. All of his books can be found on www.charlespattonbooks.com.

Charles Patton

The End

Please check out my other books at charelspattonbooks.com.

Charles Patton

www.ingramcontent.com/pod-product-compliance
Lightning Source LLC
Chambersburg PA
CBHW030254130626
46549CB00002B/528